CHINA!

Cities of China with Fun Facts

BABY PROFESSOR

EDUCATION KIDS

Speedy Publishing LLC
40 E. Main St. #1156
Newark, DE 19711
www.speedypublishing.com

Learn about CHINA!

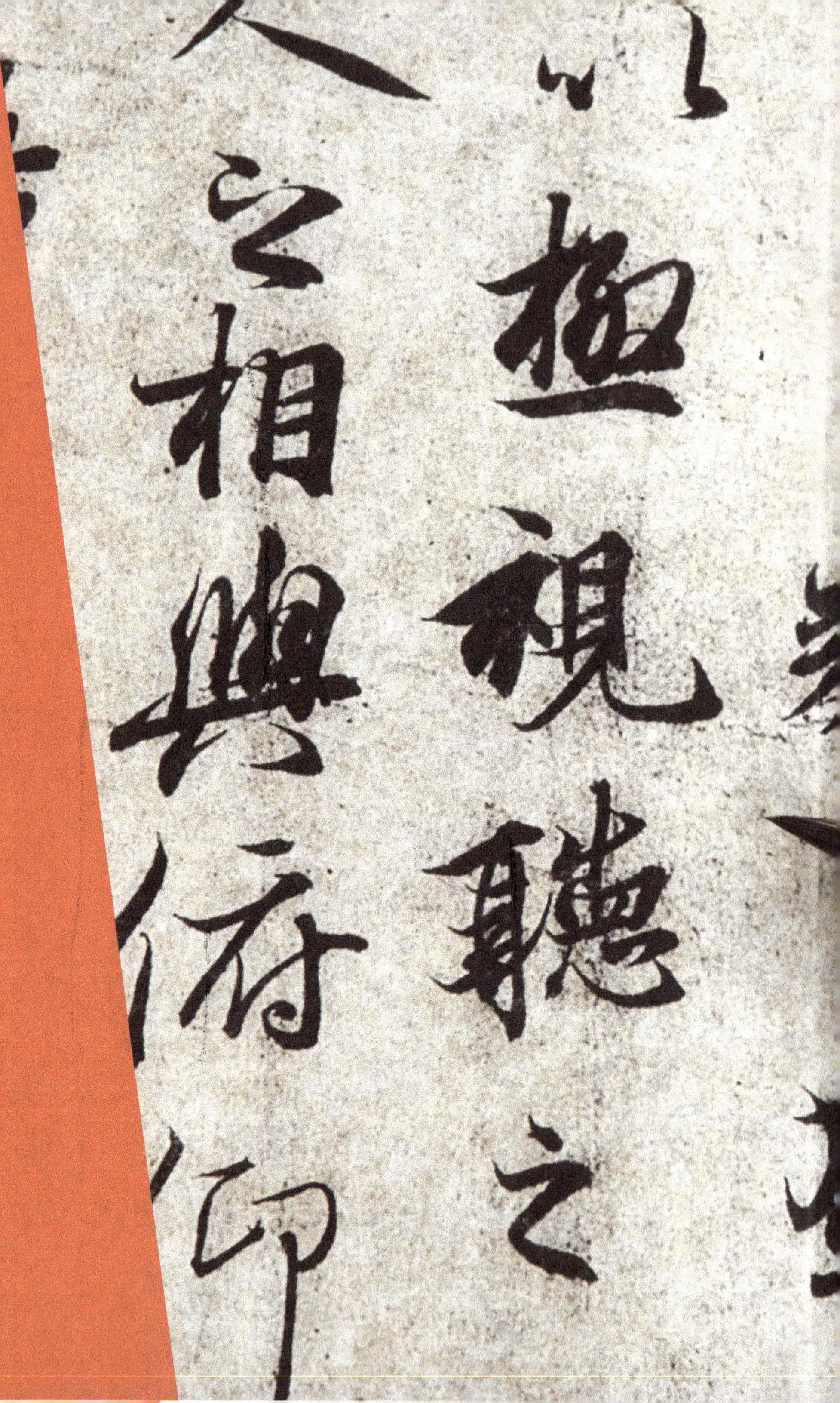

China has a very long history. China is home of one of the world's oldest civilizations. It also has the world's longest used written language.

China is the third largest country in the world. China is part of the continent of Asia. China has the second-largest economy in the world, after the United States of America.

China is officially known as the People's Republic of China. China has a surprising number of big and rapidly growing cities. China has the largest population of any country in the world, with over 1.3 billion people.

新雅
城广场
料
观光车 City Sightseeing
观光车 City Sightseeing
脉动
@随时脉
m&m's
m&m's
江海阳光集团公司
7

There are plenty of mountains, rivers, farmlands and deserts in China. The tallest mountain in the world, Mount Everest, borders China and Nepal. China has the fourth longest river in the world, the Yangtze River.

The Great Wall of China is the largest man-made structure. The wall's main purpose was defense against attacks and invasions from the north. This is one of the most popular tourist destinations in China.

In China 47% of the population live in urban areas. People in China speak many dialects of Chinese, like Mandarin, Wu, and Cantonese. Most people in China are Taoist, Buddhist or Muslim in their faith.

China is a socialist republic ruled by the Communist Party of China. The People's Republic of China was established on October 1, 1949. China's President and General Secretary of the Communist Party is Xi Jinping.

老廟黃金銀樓
老廟黃金
給您帶來好運氣
2203301
值
值

The capital
city is Beijing
and the most
populous city
is Shanghai.
Other major
cities include
Chongqing,
Shenzhen and
Guangzhou.
China's big
cities are
recognized as
the "factory
of the world".

It has modern
infrastructures,
skyscrapers
and malls. It is
very different
from the China
of just a few
years ago.
There are still
traditional
buildings and
neighborhoods
preserved.

Here are ten of China's top largest cities. Shanghai is the largest and wealthiest city in China. It is located on the Yangtze delta, along the central coast. Shanghai has the largest and busiest port.

Before it became a city, it was a small fishing village. Shanghai is known as the Pearl of the Orient and the Paris of the East. Shanghai means 'on top of the sea'.

Beijing is China's capital and is very large. Bei means northern, and jing means capital, so Beijing means the northern capital.

It is the
center of
the nation's
politics and
international
stock and
financial
exchanges.
It is also
China's
second
largest
city after
Shanghai.
It has the
world's
largest
airport.

开往劲松 ↑

Beijing is an ancient city. There are many historic sites in Beijing. The Forbidden City, part of The Great Wall of China and Tiananmen Square, located in the Forbidden City, are very popular destinations for tourists.

Tianjin is an enormous port and manufacturing center. It is located On the Bohai Gulf, in northeast China. The city has a significant history due to its key location on the Grand Canal, connecting the Yangtze and the Yellow Rivers.

Guangzhou is the capital of Guangdong province. It is also called the City of Flowers. Guangzhou is one of the three most populous cities, with Beijing and Shanghai.

Guangzhou is a powerful manufacturing city. It is located in the Pearl River delta in southeast China. Extremely large quantities of clothing, electronics, plastic goods, and toys are shipped from Guangzhou all over the world.

Shenzhen is located between Guangzhou and Hong Kong, on the Pearl River delta. It is a huge manufacturing center and is ranked fourth in China for industrial and technology products.

Dongguan is also on the Pearl River delta. It is ranked fourth in China for exports. It takes in huge numbers of rural factory workers who produce electronic items and hardware.

Taipei is the capital of Taiwan, an island nation located in the Pacific Ocean off the southeast coast of China. Its major industries are textiles and electronics. Taiwan is historically part of China, but is a separate Chinese nation.

Chengdu is an exception among large Chinese cities. It's the only city of over 7 million people not in eastern China. It is located in the Sichuan Basin, in west central China. In Chengdu, the pace of life is more relaxed compared to other large cities.

Chengdu is the largest city in mostly mountainous or arid western China. Its growth is more an outcome of the urbanization bringing the population towards the cities for work and business.

Hong Kong's official name is the Hong Kong Special Administrative Region. Its short name means Fragrant Harbor.
Its official languages are Chinese (Cantonese) and English.

Hong Kong is famous for its towering skyscrapers. Mostly 40% of the territory is actually country, parks, and nature reserves. Hiking the green trails is a favorite weekend activity.

It has historically been the world's leading city with the maximum number of Rolls-Royce luxury cars. It is considered to be the largest city in Asia for luxury goods and status symbols.

Hangzhou is one of the wealthiest cities in mainland China. Hangzhou has broad, clean, and orderly roads and a network of expressways. Everything appears to be well maintained to serve the tourist attractions.

Here are
some fun facts
about China.
The Olympic
Games held in
Beijing in 2008
were the most
expensive
games
in history.
Tea was
discovered
by a Chinese
emperor. They
considered
tea to be a
very important
part of life.

The oldest piece of paper in the world was found in China. The Chinese invented lots of things, like magnetic compass, printing, porcelain, silk and gunpowder. The first known Homo erectus, the Peking Man, was found in China.

China is the most populous country in the world with a population of over 1.3 billion.

China is also one of the fastest growing major economies in the world.